Dream Journal Diary

This Belongs To:

_ _ _ _ _ _ _ _ _ _ _ _ _ _ _ _ _ _ _

Contact Number:

_ _ _ _ _ _ _ _ _ _ _ _ _ _ _ _ _ _ _

Dedication

This Dream Journal is dedicated to all the people out there who want to write their dreams down and document their findings in the process.

You are my inspiration for producing books and I'm honored to be a part of keeping all of your dreams notes and records organized.

This journal notebook will help you record your details about your dreams.

Thoughtfully put together with these sections to record: Dream Title, Date, Characters, Location, What Happened, Emotions, Feelings, Sensations, Sketch Your Dream, Interpretation, Time Went To Bed, and much more!

How to Use this Book

The purpose of this book is to keep all of your Dream notes all in one place. It will help keep you organized.

This Night Sky Observation Book will allow you to accurately document every detail about your nightly dreams. It's a great way to chart your course through remembering your dreams.

Here are examples of the prompts for you to fill in and write about your experience in this book:

1. Dream Title, Date, Characters, Locations

2. Describe What Happened In The Dream

3. Emotions Experienced, Feelings/Sensations

4. Sketch Your Dream

5. Interpretation, Dream's Message & Importance

6. Time Went To Bed, Where Slept, Mood At Bedtime

7. Quality Of Sleep, Eaten Before Bed

8. Nighttime Notes Page (Blank Lined, Ruled)

Dream Title:

_____

Date: _____

Characters:

Locations:

Feelings/Sensations:

Describe What Happened
In the Dream:

Emotions Experienced/Felt:

Anger   Amusement   Arousal   Confusion   Courage
Envy   Guilt   Fear   Happiness   Grief   Hope   Humiliation
Love   Neutral   Paralysis   Sadness   Surprise   Panic
Vulnerability   Vengeful

Sketch What You Saw In Your Dream

Interpretation:

_____

_____

_____

_____

Dream's **Message & Importance:**

_____

_____

_____

_____

Time Went To Bed:	Where Slept:
Mood At Bedtime:	Quality Of Sleep:
Eaten Before Bed:	

Nighttime Notes:

Nighttime Notes:

Dream Title:

_____

Date: _____

Characters:

Locations:

Feelings/Sensations:

Describe What Happened
In the Dream:

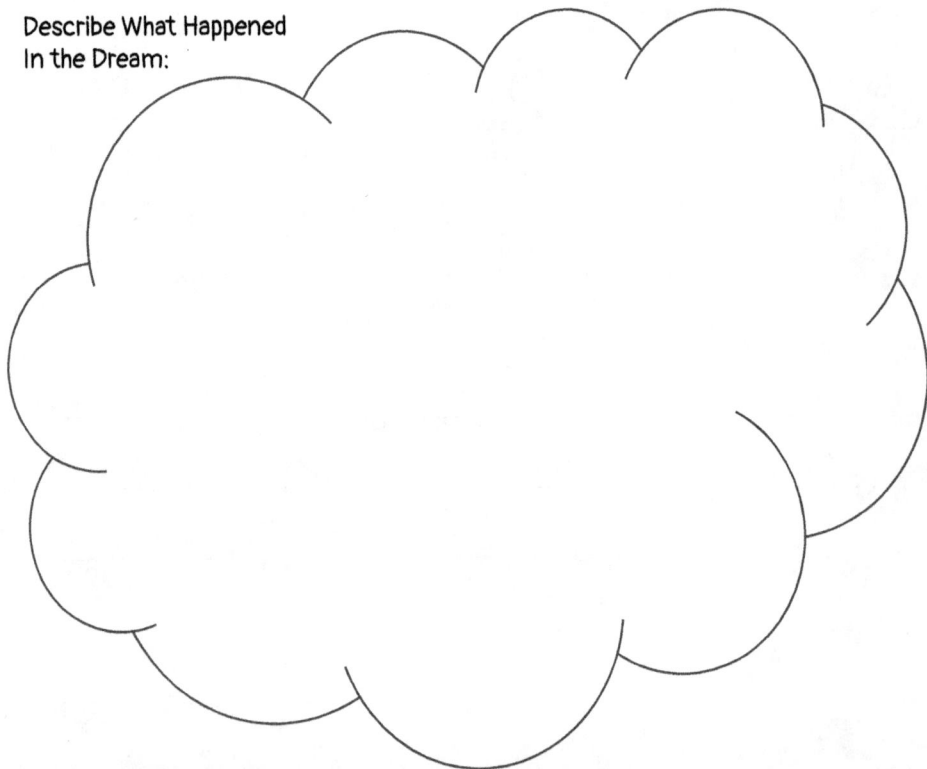

Emotions Experienced/Felt:

Anger   Amusement   Arousal   Confusion   Courage
Envy   Guilt   Fear   Happiness   Grief   Hope   Humiliation
Love   Neutral   Paralysis   Sadness   Surprise   Panic
Vulnerability   Vengeful

Sketch What You Saw In Your Dream

Interpretation:

_____

_____

_____

_____

Dream's Message & Importance:

_____

_____

_____

_____

Time Went To Bed:	Where Slept:
Mood At Bedtime:	Quality Of Sleep:
Eaten Before Bed:	

Nighttime Notes:

Nighttime Notes:

Zzz

Dream Title:

_ _ _ _ _ _ _ _ _ _ _ _ _ _ _ _ _ _ _ _

Date: _ _ _ _ _ _ _ _ _ _ _ _ _ _ _ _ _

Characters:

Locations:

Feelings/Sensations:

Describe What Happened
In the Dream:

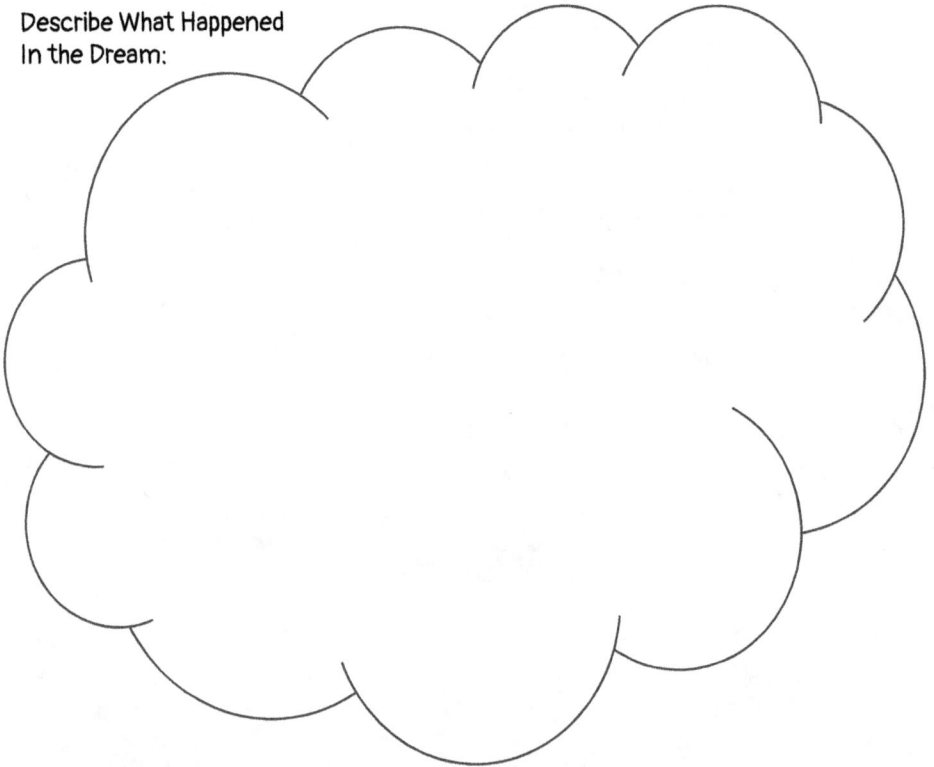

Emotions Experienced/Felt:

Anger	Amusement	Arousal	Confusion	Courage
Envy	Guilt	Fear	Happiness	Grief	Hope	Humiliation
Love	Neutral	Paralysis	Sadness	Surprise	Panic
Vulnerability	Vengeful			

Sketch What You Saw In Your Dream

Interpretation:

_____

_____

_____

_____

Dream's **Message & Importance:**

_____

_____

_____

_____

Time Went To Bed:	Where Slept:
Mood At Bedtime:	Quality Of Sleep:
Eaten Before Bed:	

Nighttime Notes:

Nighttime Notes:

Zzz

Dream Title:

- -

Date: -

Characters:

Locations:

Feelings/Sensations:

Describe What Happened
In the Dream:

Emotions Experienced/Felt:

Anger	Amusement	Arousal	Confusion	Courage
Envy	Guilt	Fear	Happiness	Grief	Hope	Humiliation
Love	Neutral	Paralysis	Sadness	Surprise	Panic
Vulnerability	Vengeful			

Sketch What You Saw In Your Dream

Interpretation:

_____

_____

_____

_____

Dream's Message & Importance:

_____

_____

_____

_____

Time Went To Bed:	Where Slept:
Mood At Bedtime:	Quality Of Sleep:
Eaten Before Bed:	

Nighttime Notes:

Nighttime Notes:

Dream Title:

- -

Date: -

Characters:

Locations:

Feelings/Sensations:

Describe What Happened
In the Dream:

Emotions Experienced/Felt:

Anger   Amusement   Arousal   Confusion   Courage
Envy   Guilt   Fear   Happiness   Grief   Hope   Humiliation
Love   Neutral   Paralysis   Sadness   Surprise   Panic
Vulnerability   Vengeful

Sketch What You Saw In Your Dream

Interpretation:

_____

_____

_____

_____

Dream's **Message & Importance:**

_____

_____

_____

_____

Time Went To Bed:	Where Slept:
Mood At Bedtime:	Quality Of Sleep:
Eaten Before Bed:	

Nighttime Notes:

Nighttime Notes:

Zzz

Dream Title:

_____

Date: _____

Characters:

Locations:

Feelings/Sensations:

Describe What Happened
In the Dream:

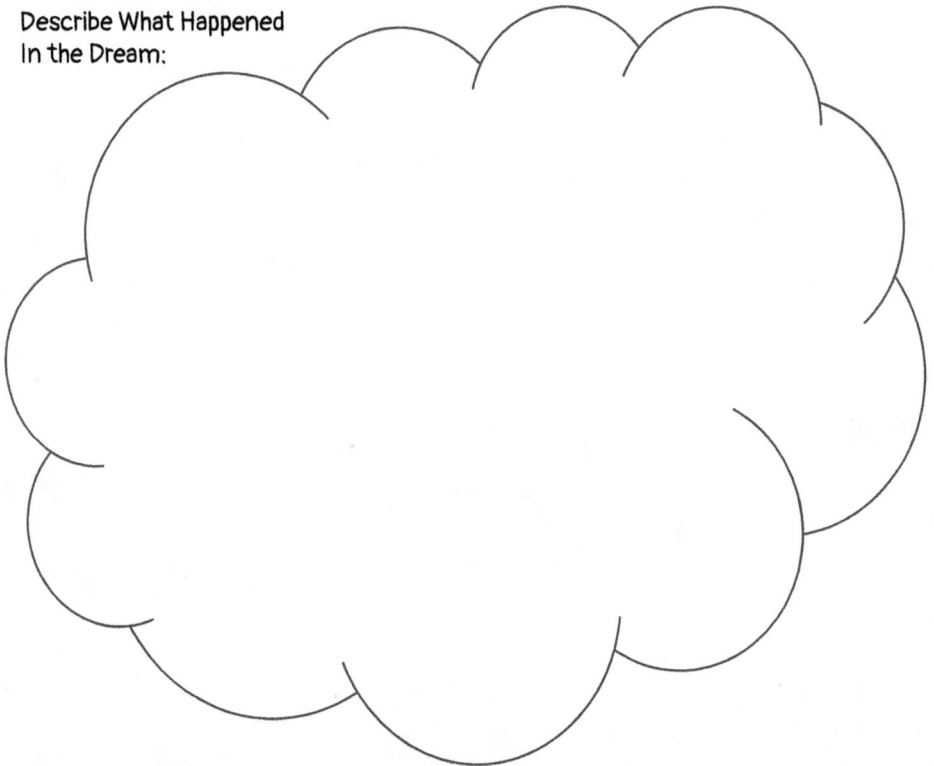

Emotions Experienced/Felt:

Anger   Amusement   Arousal   Confusion   Courage
Envy   Guilt   Fear   Happiness   Grief   Hope   Humiliation
Love   Neutral   Paralysis   Sadness   Surprise   Panic
Vulnerability   Vengeful

Sketch What You Saw In Your Dream

Interpretation:

_____

_____

_____

_____

Dream's **Message & Importance:**

_____

_____

_____

_____

Time Went To Bed:	Where Slept:
Mood At Bedtime:	Quality Of Sleep:
Eaten Before Bed:	

Nighttime Notes:

Nighttime Notes:

Zzz

Dream Title:

- -

Date: -

Characters:

Locations:

Feelings/Sensations:

Describe What Happened
In the Dream:

Emotions Experienced/Felt:
Anger   Amusement   Arousal   Confusion   Courage
Envy   Guilt   Fear   Happiness   Grief   Hope   Humiliation
Love   Neutral   Paralysis   Sadness   Surprise   Panic
Vulnerability   Vengeful

Sketch What You Saw In Your Dream

Interpretation:

_____

_____

_____

_____

Dream's **Message & Importance**:

_____

_____

_____

_____

Time Went To Bed:	Where Slept:
Mood At Bedtime:	Quality Of Sleep:
Eaten Before Bed:	

Nighttime Notes:

Nighttime Notes:

Zzz

Dream Title:

_ _

Date: _

Characters:

Locations:

Feelings/Sensations:

Describe What Happened
In the Dream:

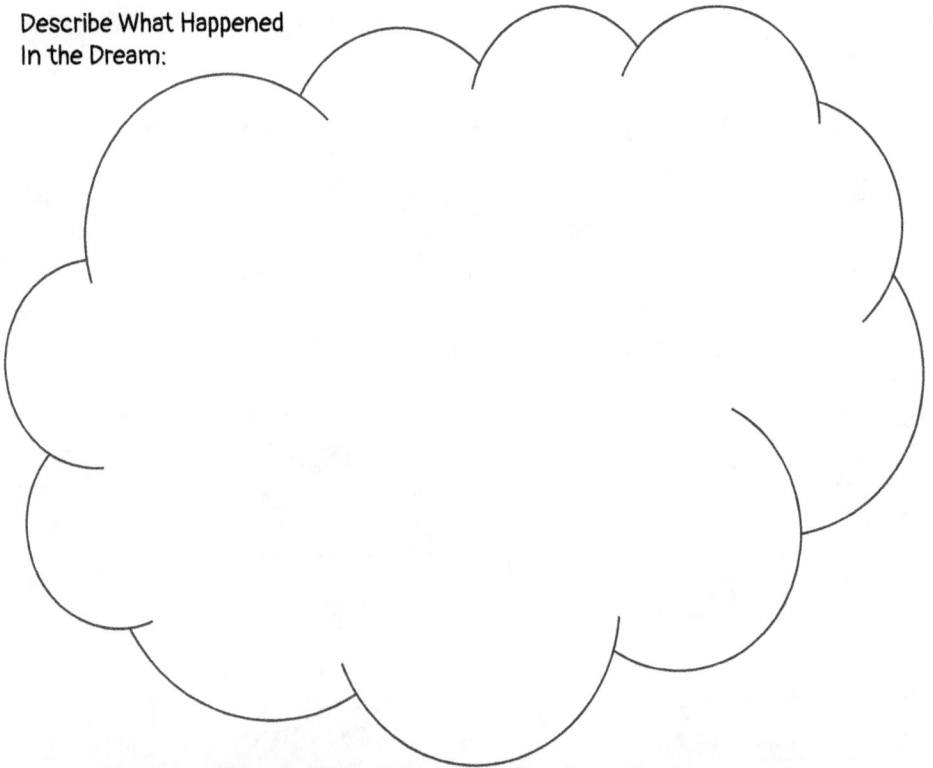

Emotions Experienced/Felt:

Anger	Amusement	Arousal	Confusion	Courage
Envy	Guilt	Fear	Happiness	Grief	Hope	Humiliation
Love	Neutral	Paralysis	Sadness	Surprise	Panic
Vulnerability	Vengeful			

Sketch What You Saw In Your Dream

Interpretation:

_____

_____

_____

_____

Dream's **Message & Importance:**

_____

_____

_____

_____

Time Went To Bed:	Where Slept:
Mood At Bedtime:	Quality Of Sleep:
Eaten Before Bed:	

Nighttime Notes:

Nighttime Notes:

Dream Title:

- -

Date: -

Characters:

Locations:

Feelings/Sensations:

Describe What Happened
In the Dream:

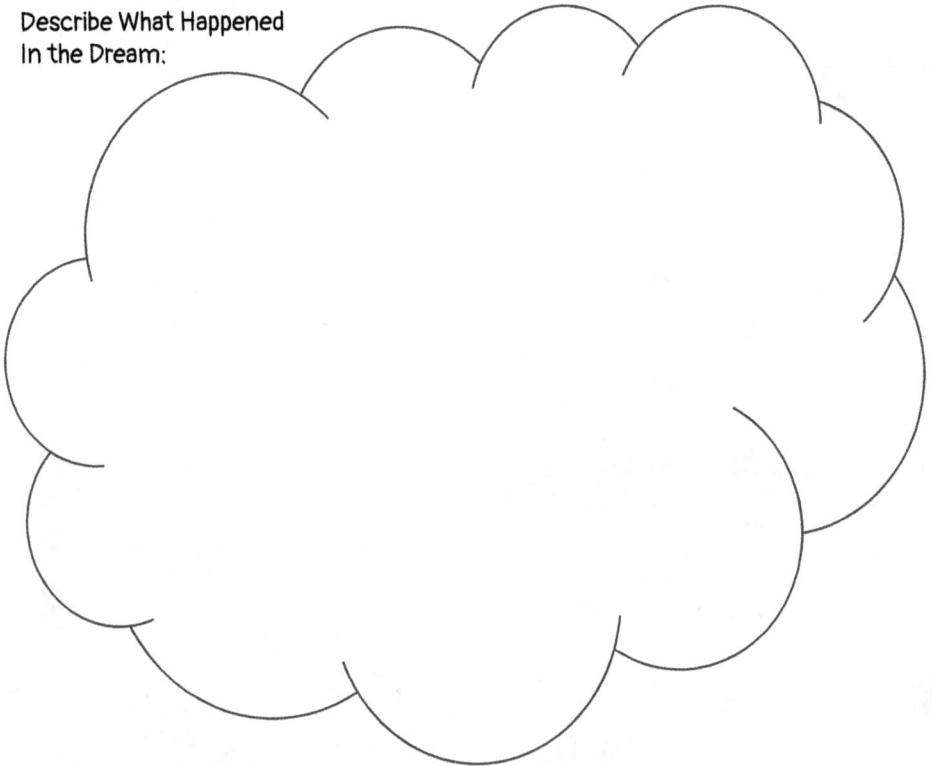

Emotions Experienced/Felt:

Anger   Amusement   Arousal   Confusion   Courage
Envy   Guilt   Fear   Happiness   Grief   Hope   Humiliation
Love   Neutral   Paralysis   Sadness   Surprise   Panic
Vulnerability   Vengeful

Sketch What You Saw In Your Dream

Interpretation:

_____

_____

_____

_____

Dream's Message & Importance:

_____

_____

_____

_____

Time Went To Bed:	Where Slept:
Mood At Bedtime:	Quality Of Sleep:
Eaten Before Bed:	

Nighttime Notes:

Nighttime Notes:

Zzz

Dream Title:

- -

Date: -

Characters:

Locations:

Feelings/Sensations:

Describe What Happened
In the Dream:

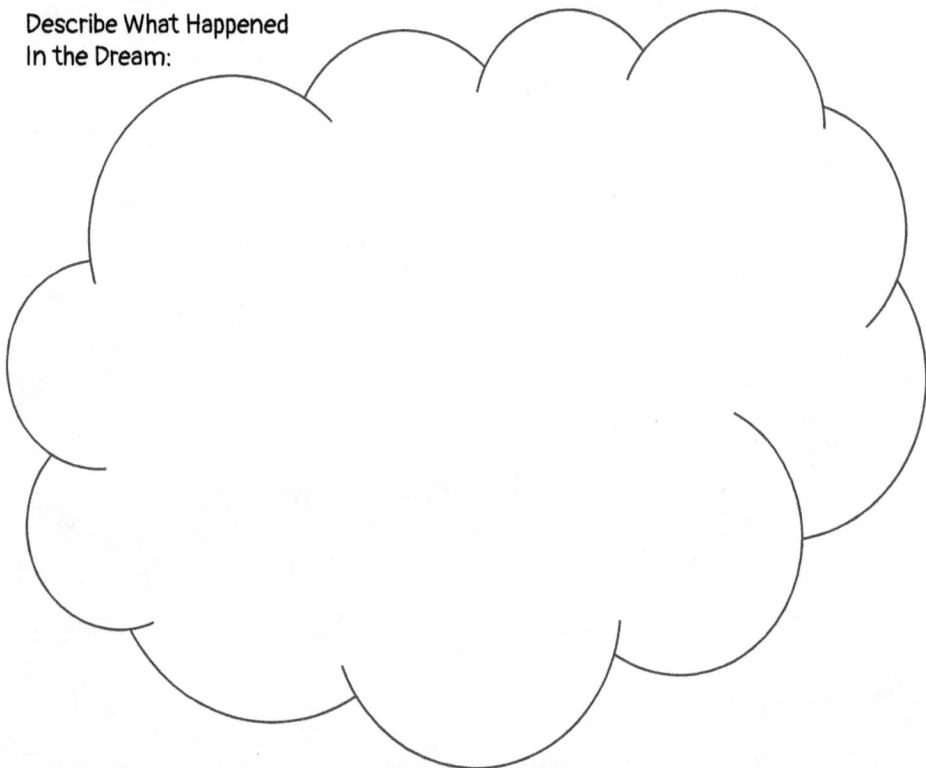

Emotions Experienced/Felt:

Anger	Amusement	Arousal	Confusion	Courage
Envy	Guilt	Fear	Happiness	Grief	Hope	Humiliation
Love	Neutral	Paralysis	Sadness	Surprise	Panic
Vulnerability	Vengeful

Sketch What You Saw In Your Dream

Interpretation:

_____

_____

_____

_____

Dream's **Message & Importance:**

_____

_____

_____

_____

Time Went To Bed:	Where Slept:
Mood At Bedtime:	Quality Of Sleep:
Eaten Before Bed:	

Nighttime Notes:

Nighttime Notes:

Dream Title:

- -

Date: -

Characters:

Locations:

Feelings/Sensations:

Describe What Happened
In the Dream:

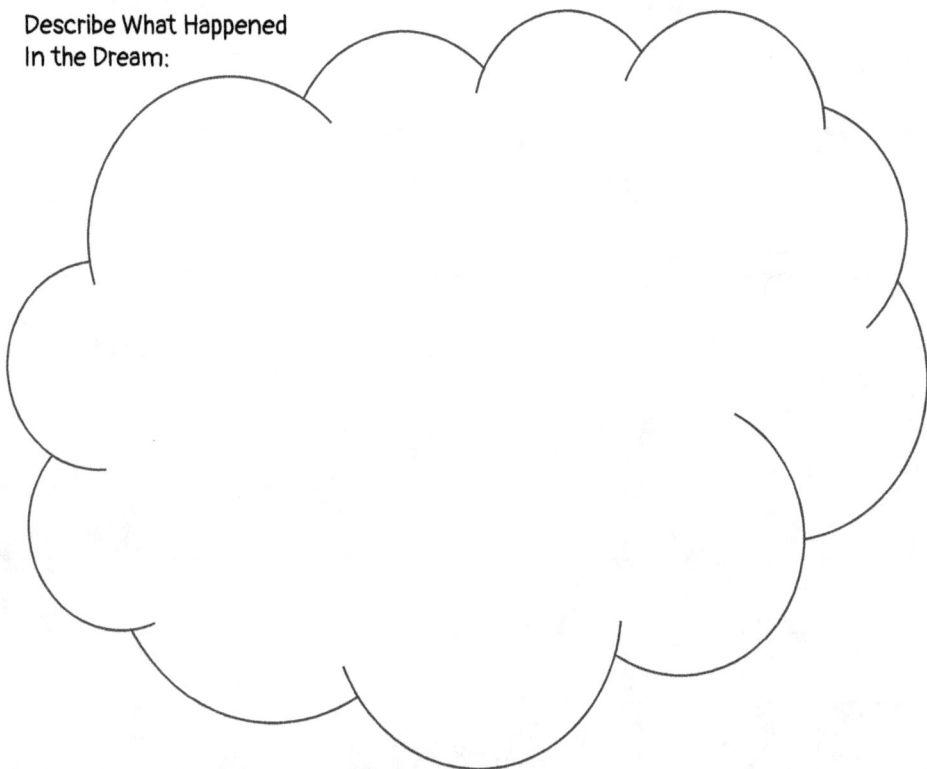

Emotions Experienced/Felt:

Anger   Amusement   Arousal   Confusion   Courage
Envy   Guilt   Fear   Happiness   Grief   Hope   Humiliation
Love   Neutral   Paralysis   Sadness   Surprise   Panic
Vulnerability   Vengeful

Sketch What You Saw In Your Dream

Interpretation:

_____

_____

_____

_____

Dream's Message & Importance:

_____

_____

_____

_____

Time Went To Bed:	Where Slept:
Mood At Bedtime:	Quality Of Sleep:
Eaten Before Bed:	

Nighttime Notes:

Nighttime Notes:

Zzz

Dream Title:

- -

Date: -

Characters:

Locations:

Feelings/Sensations:

Describe What Happened
In the Dream:

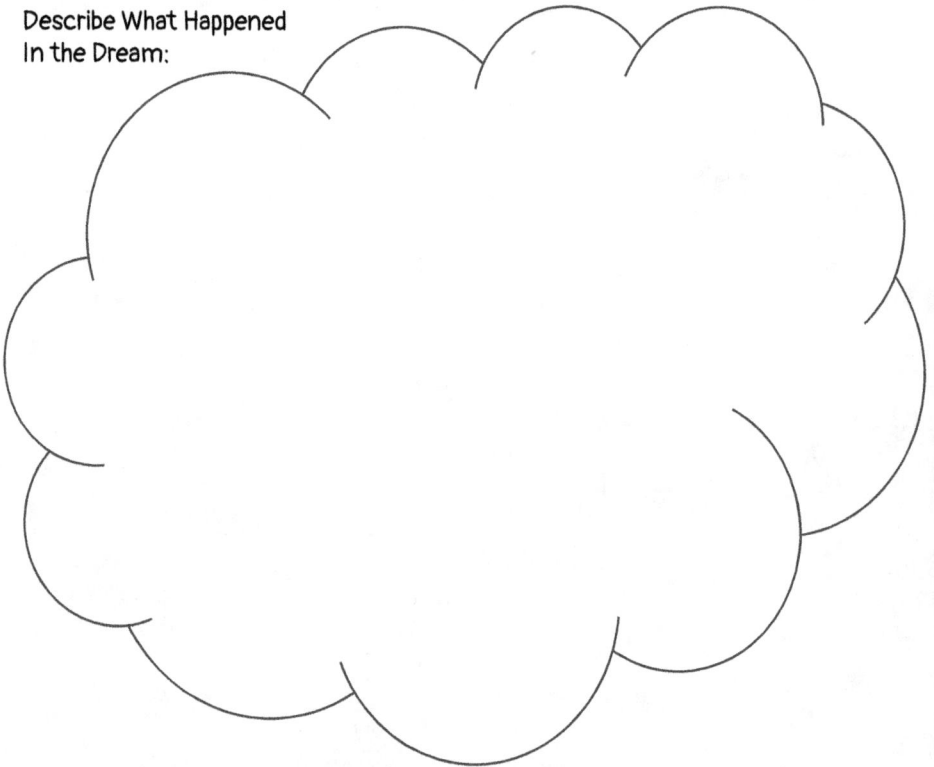

Emotions Experienced/Felt:

Anger   Amusement   Arousal   Confusion   Courage
Envy   Guilt   Fear   Happiness   Grief   Hope   Humiliation
Love   Neutral   Paralysis   Sadness   Surprise   Panic
Vulnerability   Vengeful

Sketch What You Saw In Your Dream

Interpretation:

_____

_____

_____

_____

Dream's **Message & Importance:**

_____

_____

_____

_____

Time Went To Bed:	Where Slept:
Mood At Bedtime:	Quality Of Sleep:
Eaten Before Bed:	

Nighttime Notes:

Nighttime Notes:

Zzz

Dream Title:

- -

Date: -

Characters:

Locations:

Feelings/Sensations:

Describe What Happened
In the Dream:

Emotions Experienced/Felt:

Anger   Amusement   Arousal   Confusion   Courage
Envy   Guilt   Fear   Happiness   Grief   Hope   Humiliation
Love   Neutral   Paralysis   Sadness   Surprise   Panic
Vulnerability   Vengeful

Sketch What You Saw In Your Dream

Interpretation:

_____

_____

_____

_____

Dream's **Message & Importance:**

_____

_____

_____

_____

Time Went To Bed:	Where Slept:
Mood At Bedtime:	Quality Of Sleep:
Eaten Before Bed:	

Nighttime Notes:

Nighttime Notes:

Dream Title:

_____

Date: _____

Characters:

Locations:

Feelings/Sensations:

Describe What Happened
In the Dream:

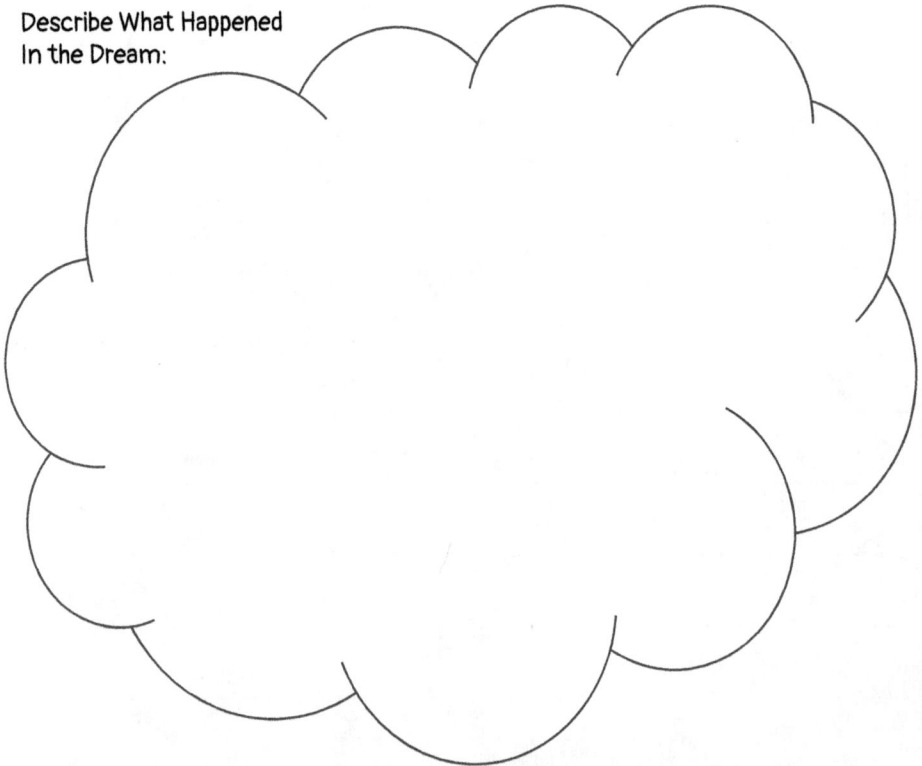

Emotions Experienced/Felt:
Anger   Amusement   Arousal   Confusion   Courage
Envy   Guilt   Fear   Happiness   Grief   Hope   Humiliation
Love   Neutral   Paralysis   Sadness   Surprise   Panic
Vulnerability   Vengeful

Sketch What You Saw In Your Dream

Interpretation:

_____

_____

_____

_____

Dream's Message & Importance:

_____

_____

_____

_____

Time Went To Bed:	Where Slept:
Mood At Bedtime:	Quality Of Sleep:
Eaten Before Bed:	

Nighttime Notes:

Nighttime Notes:

Zzz

Dream Title:

_ _

Date: _

Characters:

Locations:

Feelings/Sensations:

Describe What Happened
In the Dream:

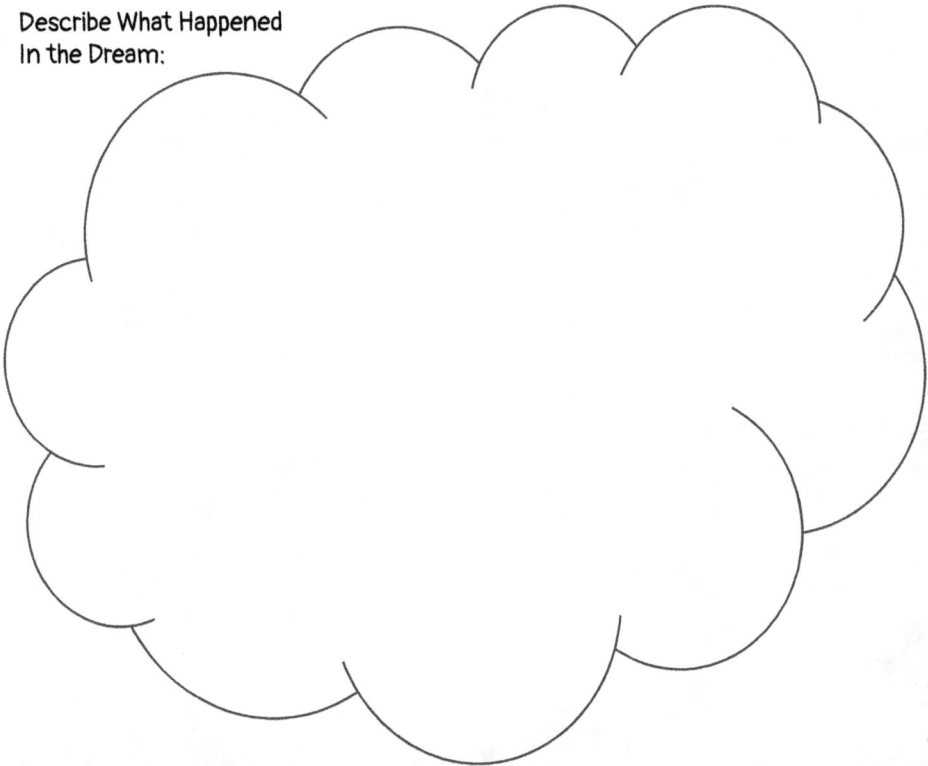

Emotions Experienced/Felt:
Anger   Amusement   Arousal   Confusion   Courage
Envy   Guilt   Fear   Happiness   Grief   Hope   Humiliation
Love   Neutral   Paralysis   Sadness   Surprise   Panic
Vulnerability   Vengeful

Sketch What You Saw In Your Dream

Interpretation:

_____

_____

_____

_____

Dream's Message & Importance:

_____

_____

_____

_____

Time Went To Bed:	Where Slept:
Mood At Bedtime:	Quality Of Sleep:
Eaten Before Bed:	

Nighttime Notes:

Nighttime Notes:

Dream Title:

_____

Date: _____

Characters:

Locations:

Feelings/Sensations:

Describe What Happened
In the Dream:

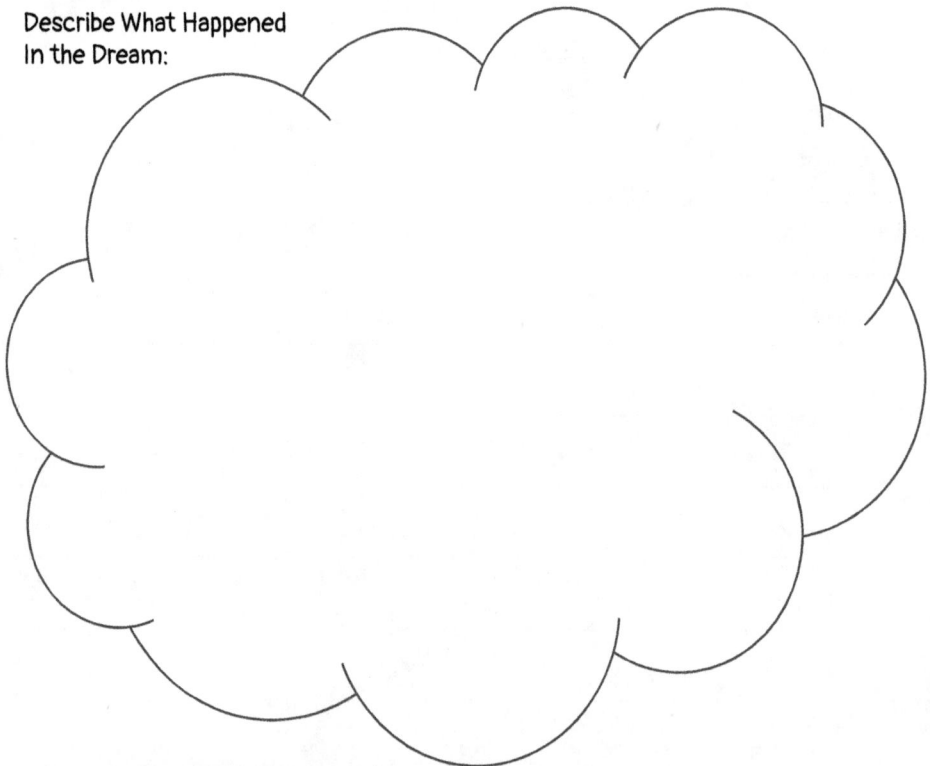

Emotions Experienced/Felt:

Anger   Amusement   Arousal   Confusion   Courage
Envy   Guilt   Fear   Happiness   Grief   Hope   Humiliation
Love   Neutral   Paralysis   Sadness   Surprise   Panic
Vulnerability   Vengeful

Sketch What You Saw In Your Dream

Interpretation:

_____

_____

_____

_____

Dream's Message & Importance:

_____

_____

_____

_____

Time Went To Bed:	Where Slept:
Mood At Bedtime:	Quality Of Sleep:
Eaten Before Bed:	

Nighttime Notes:

Nighttime Notes:

Zzz

Dream Title:

_ _

Date: _

Characters:

Locations:

Feelings/Sensations:

Describe What Happened
In the Dream:

Emotions Experienced/Felt:

Anger	Amusement	Arousal	Confusion	Courage
Envy	Guilt	Fear	Happiness	Grief	Hope	Humiliation
Love	Neutral	Paralysis	Sadness	Surprise	Panic
Vulnerability	Vengeful			

Sketch What You Saw In Your Dream

Interpretation:

_____

_____

_____

_____

Dream's **Message & Importance:**

_____

_____

_____

_____

Time Went To Bed:	Where Slept:
Mood At Bedtime:	Quality Of Sleep:
Eaten Before Bed:	

Nighttime Notes:

Nighttime Notes:

Zzz

Dream Title:

_ _

Date: _

Characters:

Locations:

Feelings/Sensations:

Describe What Happened
In the Dream:

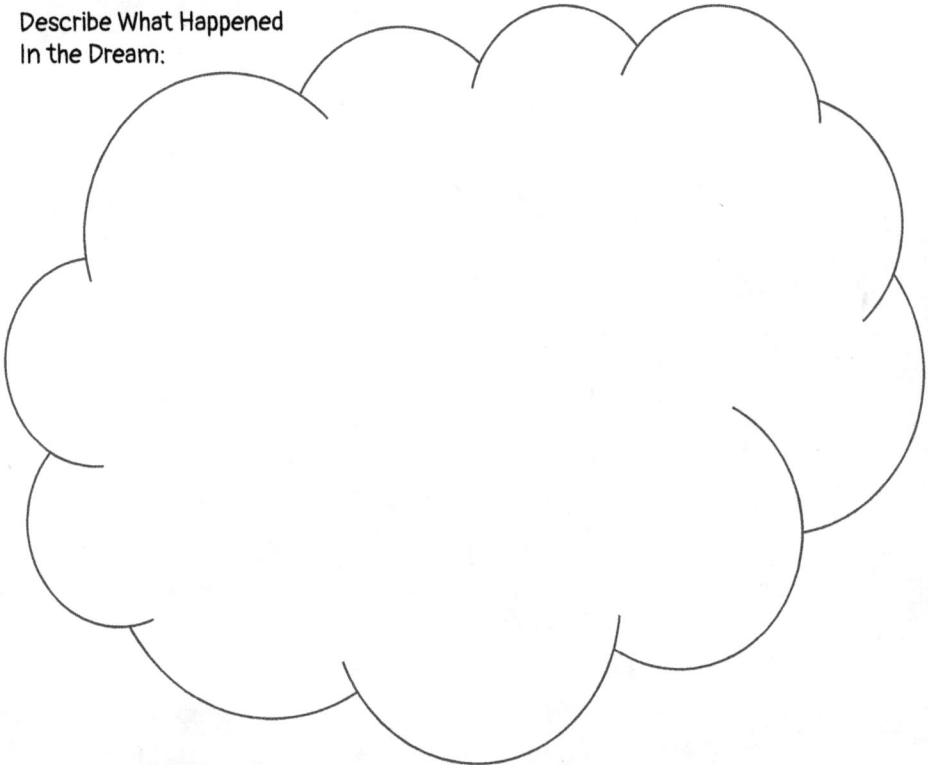

Emotions Experienced/Felt:
Anger   Amusement   Arousal   Confusion   Courage
Envy   Guilt   Fear   Happiness   Grief   Hope   Humiliation
Love   Neutral   Paralysis   Sadness   Surprise   Panic
Vulnerability   Vengeful

Sketch What You Saw In Your Dream

Interpretation:

_____

_____

_____

_____

Dream's Message & Importance:

_____

_____

_____

_____

Time Went To Bed:	Where Slept:
Mood At Bedtime:	Quality Of Sleep:
Eaten Before Bed:	

Nighttime Notes:

Nighttime Notes:

Zzz

Dream Title:

- -

Date: -

Characters:

Locations:

Feelings/Sensations:

Describe What Happened
In the Dream:

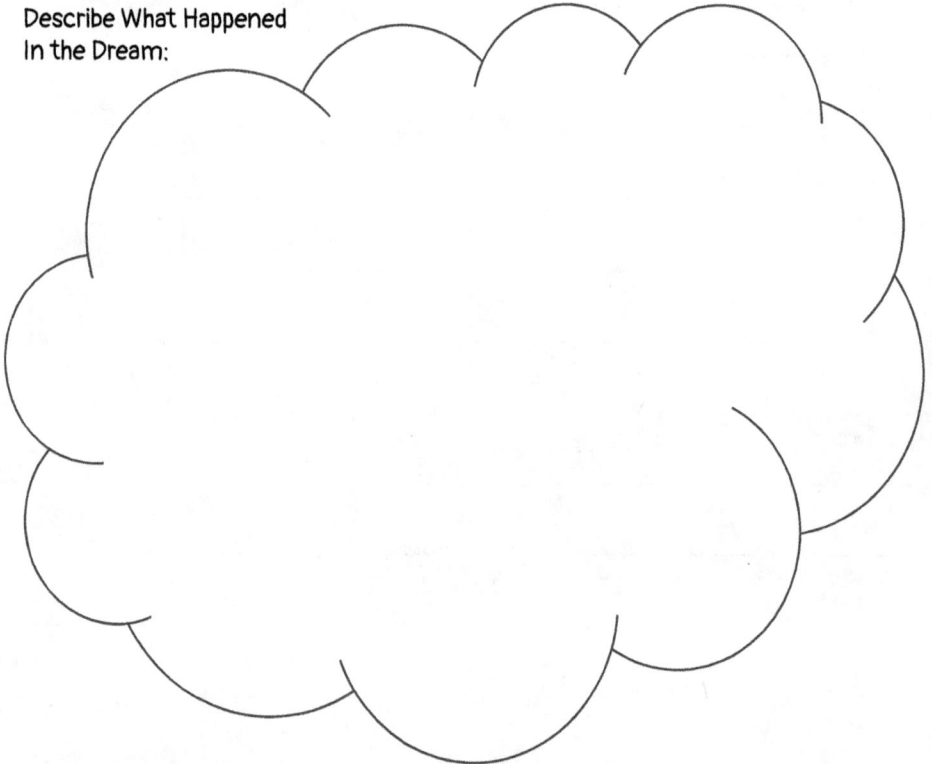

Emotions Experienced/Felt:

Anger   Amusement   Arousal   Confusion   Courage

Envy   Guilt   Fear   Happiness   Grief   Hope   Humiliation

Love   Neutral   Paralysis   Sadness   Surprise   Panic

Vulnerability   Vengeful

Sketch What You Saw In Your Dream

Interpretation:

_____

_____

_____

_____

Dream's Message & Importance:

_____

_____

_____

_____

Time Went To Bed:	Where Slept:
Mood At Bedtime:	Quality Of Sleep:
Eaten Before Bed:	

Nighttime Notes:

Nighttime Notes:

Dream Title:

- -

Date: -

Characters:

Locations:

Feelings/Sensations:

Describe What Happened
In the Dream:

Emotions Experienced/Felt:

Anger   Amusement   Arousal   Confusion   Courage
Envy   Guilt   Fear   Happiness   Grief   Hope   Humiliation
Love   Neutral   Paralysis   Sadness   Surprise   Panic
Vulnerability   Vengeful

Sketch What You Saw In Your Dream

Interpretation:

_____

_____

_____

_____

Dream's **Message & Importance:**

_____

_____

_____

_____

Time Went To Bed:	Where Slept:
Mood At Bedtime:	Quality Of Sleep:
Eaten Before Bed:	

Nighttime Notes:

Nighttime Notes:

Zzz

Dream Title:

_ _

Date: _

Characters:

Locations:

Feelings/Sensations:

Describe What Happened
In the Dream:

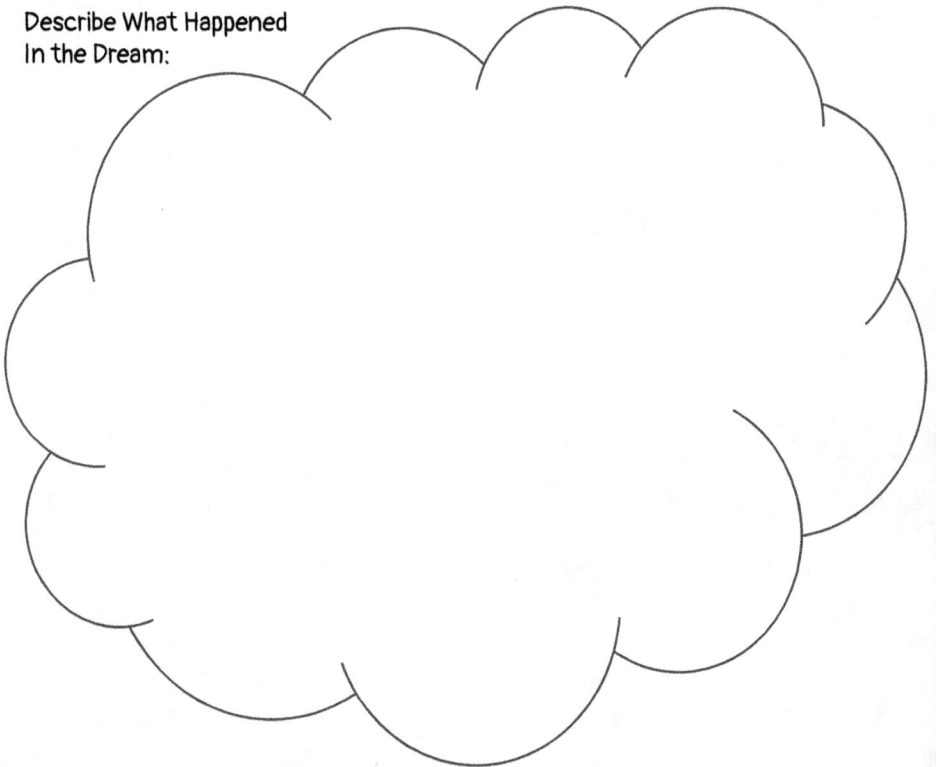

Emotions Experienced/Felt:

Anger   Amusement   Arousal   Confusion   Courage
Envy   Guilt   Fear   Happiness   Grief   Hope   Humiliation
Love   Neutral   Paralysis   Sadness   Surprise   Panic
Vulnerability   Vengeful

Sketch What You Saw In Your Dream

Interpretation:

_____

_____

_____

_____

Dream's **Message & Importance:**

_____

_____

_____

_____

Time Went To Bed:	Where Slept:
Mood At Bedtime:	Quality Of Sleep:
Eaten Before Bed:	

Nighttime Notes:

Nighttime Notes:

Dream Title:

Date: -------------------------------

Characters:

Locations:

Feelings/Sensations:

Describe What Happened
In the Dream:

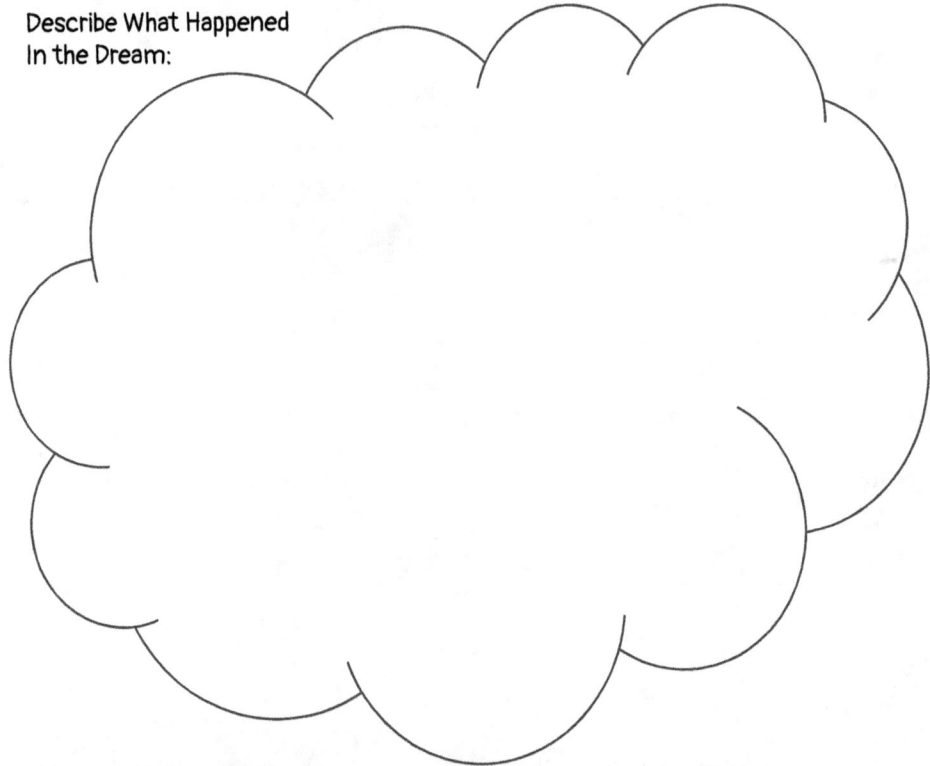

Emotions Experienced/Felt:

Anger	Amusement	Arousal	Confusion	Courage
Envy	Guilt	Fear	Happiness	Grief	Hope	Humiliation
Love	Neutral	Paralysis	Sadness	Surprise	Panic
Vulnerability	Vengeful			

Sketch What You Saw In Your Dream

Interpretation:

_____

_____

_____

_____

Dream's **Message & Importance:**

_____

_____

_____

_____

Time Went To Bed:	Where Slept:
Mood At Bedtime:	Quality Of Sleep:
Eaten Before Bed:	

Nighttime Notes:

Nighttime Notes:

Dream Title:

\- -

Date: -

Characters:

Locations:

Feelings/Sensations:

Describe What Happened
In the Dream:

Emotions Experienced/Felt:

Anger	Amusement	Arousal	Confusion	Courage
Envy	Guilt	Fear	Happiness	Grief	Hope	Humiliation
Love	Neutral	Paralysis	Sadness	Surprise	Panic
Vulnerability	Vengeful

Sketch What You Saw In Your Dream

Interpretation:

_____

_____

_____

_____

Dream's **Message & Importance:**

_____

_____

_____

_____

Time Went To Bed:	Where Slept:
Mood At Bedtime:	Quality Of Sleep:
Eaten Before Bed:	

Nighttime Notes:

Nighttime Notes:

Zzz

Dream Title:

_____

Date: _____

Characters:

Locations:

Feelings/Sensations:

Describe What Happened
In the Dream:

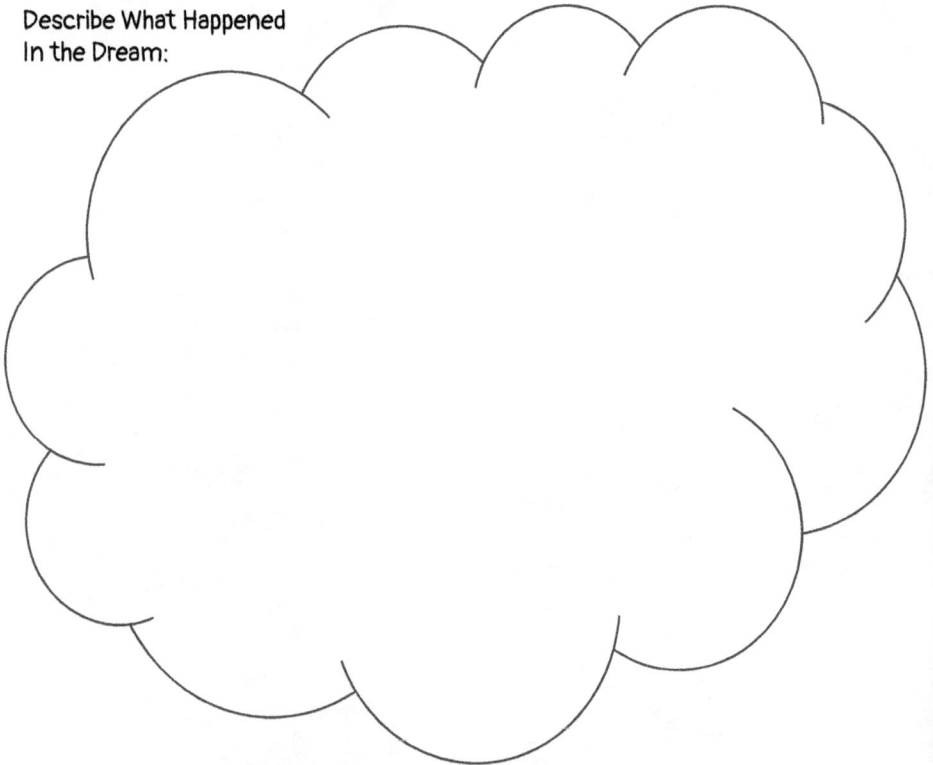

Emotions Experienced/Felt:

Anger   Amusement   Arousal   Confusion   Courage
Envy   Guilt   Fear   Happiness   Grief   Hope   Humiliation
Love   Neutral   Paralysis   Sadness   Surprise   Panic
Vulnerability   Vengeful

Sketch What You Saw In Your Dream

Interpretation:

_____

_____

_____

_____

Dream's Message & Importance:

_____

_____

_____

_____

Time Went To Bed:	Where Slept:
Mood At Bedtime:	Quality Of Sleep:
Eaten Before Bed:	

Nighttime Notes:

Nighttime Notes:

Zzz

Dream Title:

_ _

Date: _ _ _ _ _ _ _ _ _ _ _ _ _ _ _ _ _ _

Characters:

Locations:

Feelings/Sensations:

Describe What Happened
In the Dream:

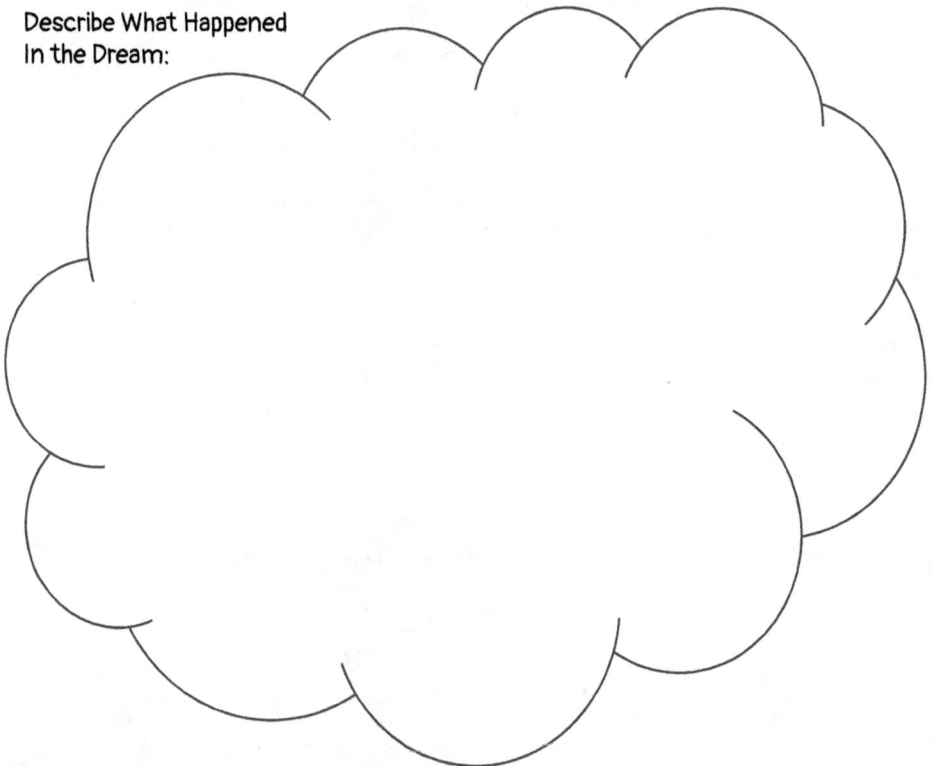

Emotions Experienced/Felt:

Anger	Amusement	Arousal	Confusion	Courage
Envy	Guilt	Fear	Happiness	Grief	Hope	Humiliation
Love	Neutral	Paralysis	Sadness	Surprise	Panic
Vulnerability	Vengeful

Sketch What You Saw In Your Dream

Interpretation:

_____

_____

_____

_____

Dream's **Message & Importance:**

_____

_____

_____

_____

Time Went To Bed:	Where Slept:
Mood At Bedtime:	Quality Of Sleep:
Eaten Before Bed:	

Nighttime Notes:

Nighttime Notes:

www.ingramcontent.com/pod-product-compliance
Lightning Source LLC
Chambersburg PA
CBHW051031030426
42336CB00015B/2828